SONG OF PROTEST

Song of Protest

by Pablo Neruda

Translated and with an Introduction by Miguel Algarín

William Morrow and Company, Inc.
New York   1976

Originally published in Spanish by Editorial El Siglo Ilustrado, Montevideo, under the title, *Canción de Gesta*, copyright by Editorial El Siglo Ilustrado.

Printed in the United States of America.

1 2 3 4 5   80 79 78 77 76

Library of Congress Cataloging in Publication Data

Neruda, Pablo, 1904-1973.
    Song of protest.

    Translation of Canción de gesta.
    1. Latin America—History—20th century—Poetry.
    2. Poetry of places—Latin America. I. Title.
PQ8097.N4C1513   821   75-45216
ISBN 0-688-03043-2

Book design: H. Roberts

Dedicated to
Richard August
Jorge Rodriguez-Colon, for his help in my work
Miguel Piñero
Lucky CienFuegos
& the Young Nuyorican Poets

M.A.

Contents

Introduction: The Politics of Poetry
   by Miguel Algarín   9
Prefaces   35
I   Puerto Rico, Puerto Pobre   39
II   Muñoz Marín   40
III   It Is Happening   41
IV   Cuba Appears   43
V   The Challenge   44
VI   Ancient History   46
VII   Mid-Land   47
VIII   Also in the Distant South   49
IX   I Remember a Man   50
X   That Friend   51
XI   Treason   53
XII   Death   54
XIII   The Traitor Dies   55
XIV   Monarchs   56
XV   I Come from the South   57
XVI   In Guatemala   59
XVII   In Salvador, Death   60
XVIII   Liberty   61
XIX   To Fidel Castro   63
XX   Returning to Puerto Pobre   65
XXI   The Ambush   67
XXII   So Is My Life   68
XXIII   For Venezuela   69
XXIV   The Tiger   71
XXV   Pérez Jiménez   72
XXVI   A Strange Democrat   74
XXVII   Caribbean Birds   76
XXVIII   Mean Events   79
XXIX   Do Not Ask Me   80
XXX   OAS Meeting   82
XXXI   The Explosion of "La Coubre" 1960   84

XXXII	Americas	86
XXXIII	History of a Canal	88
XXXIV	Future of a Canal	90
XXXV	The Free "Press"	92
XXXVI	Dancing with Blacks	95
XXXVII	A Professor Disappears	97
XXXVIII	The Heroes	99
XXXIX	North American Friend	100
XL	Tomorrow Throughout the Caribbean	103
XLI	A Song for Sierra Maestra	104
XLII	Written in the Year 2000	107
XLIII	Final Judgment	113
	Pablo Neruda's Funeral	114
	Notes	117

SONG OF PROTEST

INTRODUCTION
The Politics of Poetry
by Miguel Algarín

I EVENTS

When I was a child, I trusted my mother completely.
Whenever she felt safe, I felt safe. I remember looking out for
my mother's signals. I was always alert for signals of fear. I
always looked to my parents to explain how things worked,
and they always responded to my questions. Luis Muñoz
Marín was governor of Puerto Rico when I was a child. I
remember how once my brother and sister were held up above
the head of the crowd to see Luis Muñoz Marín exit from a
radio station where he had been making a speech. My mother
was filled with electrical joy. My father stood gently still and
full of pride. But I was very sad because my uncle had decided
that I was too fat to sit on his shoulders. As the governor
exited, a furious clapping of hands was heard. So exciting was
the clapping that I forgot my sadness and began to applaud,
though all I could see were his polished white shoes.

I remember how much respect the whole family had for
Mr. Muñoz Marín. Once there was a bloody fight between my
Uncle Benitín and our next-door neighbor who kept insisting
that Mr. Muñoz Marín was selling us out. It was a puzzling
experience. I had never seen my Uncle Benitín so nettled. It
was as if a bee had stung him and he couldn't shake the pain.
Uncle Benitín leaped at the man's throat and tried to kill him.
Both families ran to the rescue, the men were separated,
everybody cooled down, but the men never spoke to each other
again. Overall, Mr. Muñoz Marín was, however, much more
loved and respected than detested.

My family moved to New York City, so Mr. Muñoz
Marín faded into the background of my mind as the new
environment began to dominate my senses. I thought about

9

the island, but its leaders and its politics left my memory's sight. Feelings about the past were encouraged, but not on the bad side. All that the family ever talked about when they got together were the good times. Rarely were the painful times brought up. A very mellow and partially ideal image of the past began to develop.

I had to cope with myself on the streets of New York before I could concentrate on the historical events that had been or were developing in Puerto Rico. I focused my entire attention on New York until I learned to survive. Soon, however, I felt dissatisfied. It was not enough to have the new. I needed a history as well. I needed my memories, and for that I needed Spanish back. I looked to the Caribbean and South American writers to feed me feelings so that I could tap my faded memory.

It was then that I found Pablo Neruda's *Song of Protest*. I was on the prowl for clear images. It had become clearer to me that Mr. Muñoz Marín was not a shining knight. But my questions about him at home flustered and after a while embarrassed and demoralized the family. I stopped asking, but in Mr. Neruda I found a teacher-friend. He wanted to tell me the events. He wanted to tell the truth so clearly that the poems he wrought are communications that seep into the neurological cells and nourish by arousing and nurturing the memory. Neruda's verbal images are chemical messages that change the body's composition.

It was really simple. I was looking to be taught and Neruda wanted to teach, and as soon as I found Neruda, I brought him home:

> There is a fat worm in these waters
> in these lands a predatory worm:
> he ate the island's flag
> hoisting up his overseer's banner,
> he was nourished from the captive blood
> of the poor buried patriots.
> ("Muñoz Marín," Poem II)

" 'A fat worm'—that's a corrupted image from a corrupted poet," my Uncle Al shouted. The struggle was not easy. The reaction at home was definitive, "The poet of these poems is forgetting the business of poetry." My Uncle Al was aroused to aggression. I remember that he swung at me, flipping the table, the book, and me onto the floor. I kept insisting that it was "only a poem," and he shouted at me that it wasn't just a poem, that it was the devil trying to destroy the image of a good and righteous ruler. I was hurt and glad at Uncle Al's response. It was clear that Neruda's poems were hitting right smack in the middle of Uncle Al's stored-up pain. I stopped reading for that day.

I have heard poems read in public that have been praised for their beauty and structure but which cease to provoke responses beyond a few minutes after they are read. Not so with the poems in *Song of Protest.* These poems remain in action long after their reading is over. Neruda planned it that way:

> On the golden crown of American wheat
> the worm grew fat in a maggot heap
> prospering in the monied shade,
> bloodied with tortures and soldiers,
> inaugurating false monuments,
> making the native soil inherited
> by their fathers an enslaved clod,
> making an island as transparent as a star
> into a small grave for slaves . . .
> ("Muñoz Marín," II)

There were no names too sacred or too powerful to reveal. Neruda was conscious of his task. He had set out to infuse with life the historical events of the last fifty years. Even if it meant disillusioning whole generations of people, Neruda sought to bring what had been happening (the past) directly into the actual (the present).

11

The historical event continues to be of significance only when it is remembered. However, the memory fades if there are no reminders. If my Uncle Al had never heard Neruda's poem read, perhaps he would never have examined his memories of Luis Muñoz Marín.

The pain was strong. I had learned to love and trust my family. Now I was reevaluating their information. I had to reach them. And the crisis was major. I had grown to trust all that my parents trusted, but now I could not. I began to learn about how their "facts" were given to them. I discovered that the bulk of the campaign propaganda of El Partido Popular as led by Mr. Muñoz Marín was commonplace cosmetic, industrial, democratic deceptions. I learned to cope with Mr. Muñoz Marín's lies, but I could not so easily get over understanding that my parents had been without political or economic insight and that all of the values of my childhood were false. My parents were victims of distorted, selected information. Nevertheless, their values were false and they did not awaken to the fact that it was up to them to confront the historical events of their lives.

Neruda makes you deal with the events of a past that is yours. History is personalized. It is attached to the individual. History, made concrete and contemporary, nourishes the memory of the individual and of the whole nation. It is a passionate process and the tensions are intense. A well-told tale of forgotten tyrannies can revolutionize feelings and straighten out the lies of the past.

Luis Muñoz Marín was a public ruler, and around every public ruler there is always a historical accounting of the events that took place. However, when a ruler grasps all forms of communications (newspapers, radio, TV) and destroys all objective accounting of events, someone must confront his historical account and present another. Neruda assigned himself that task in *Song of Protest*. It was his intention to create unsettling and, whenever he felt it necessary, incendiary imagery:

12

and his palace was white outside
and inside it was infernal like Chicago
with the mustache, the heart, the claws
of that traitor, of Luis Muñoz the worm,
Muñoz Marín to the people,
Judas of the blood-let land,
overseer of the enslavement of the island,
corrupter of his poor brothers,
bilingual translator for the executioners,
chauffeur of North American whiskey.

> ("Muñoz Marín," II)

The chemistry of this passage can change learned habits. If
you believe in Mr. Muñoz Marín, it arrests you because it
makes you angry and it also precipitates you into violent
confrontation with the poet. The poet engages himself to an
extreme and the reader has no choice but to respond in the
extreme as well. It is a powerful device full of rich and painful
consequences.

As I acquired information, I tried to bring it home to
my family. But my consciousness was not complete. I became
angry at the fact that my parents had not known. My Uncle Al
must have felt my intentional insult to him as I read Neruda's
poem. Instead of using the poem as a vehicle of illumination, I
used it as a weapon of offense, an accusation:

meanwhile Muñoz of Puerto Rico
falsifies his island's signature
and under the pirate's banner
he sells out language and reason, lands, and delight,
sells our poor America's honor,
sells parents and grandparents and ashes.

> ("It Is Happening," III)

When there is no distance between the past and the
present, the moment is thick with a sense of immediacy. It is
like standing on the street and catching out of the corner of
the eye a man who mugged you two months ago. Many

intentions flood the mind. Revenge. Rush him. Cool it. He's armed. Call a cop. Push him in front of the First Avenue bus. Approach him and talk him into penitence. Run away. Call for help. It goes on and on until he is out of sight and the past and the present are not in perfect conjunction. Your mind reviews the shoving, the pushing, and the fear that his cold steel blade aroused in your heart, but by the time you reach Second Avenue, the present is going rampant and the past fades out of sight though it still evokes fear.

Neruda's poems have the power to jolt the memory in exactly the same way that it is jolted by the man who robbed you. The poems bring you Neruda's images as an offering of love; the thief came and took, Neruda comes and gives, but his gift is not one of mild fragrances from the east or west. It is a gift armed to give you a memory. In "Ancient History," he leaves Puerto Rico and moves on to Cuba, where he describes an island full of wholesome natural beauty. Here is an image of what was:

> Now I open my eyes and I remember:
> it sparkles and dims, electric and dark,
> with joys and suffering
> the bitter and magic history of Cuba.
> Years passed as fish pass
> through the blue of the sea and its sweetness,
> the island lived in liberty and dance,
> the palm trees danced with the foam,
> Blacks and Whites were a single loaf of bread
> because Martí kneaded their ferment,
> peace fulfilled its destiny of gold
> and the sun crackled in the sugar,
> while ripened by the sun fell
> a beam of honey over the fruit:
> man was content with his reign
> and the family with its agriculture . . .
>
> ("Ancient History," VI)

14

It was not a perfect past. But among its imperfections there lived an image maker, José Martí, and his words had changed racial hatred and had blended mutinous wills into one. However, the local beauty "ripened by the sun" was soon to be raped:

> when from the North arrived a seed
> threatening, covetous, unjust,
> that like a spider spread her threads
> extending a metallic structure
> that drove bloodied nails into the land
> raising over the dead a vault.
> It was the dollar with its yellow teeth,
> commandant of blood and grave.
>   ("Ancient History," VI)

Marti saw the betrayal and moved against a "dollar" morality in Cuba. He faced a violent foe. It was "hard and dark work / to lift an independent laurel: / to dream of liberty was danger." (IX) Neruda wrote about men who worked out with the problems of the present. Men who confronted destructive authority gave Neruda hope and for these men he wrote songs that celebrated their deeds because he saw their courage:

> but Martí with hope and gunfire
> awakened the daydreamer and the peasant
> building with blood and thought
> the architecture of the new light.
>   ("I Remember a Man," IX)

But their courage was always betrayed.

The betrayal was possible from any direction. In Nicaragua, Augusto C. Sandino "unloaded his sacred gunpowder / against assaulting sailors / grown and paid for in New York." (X) His struggle brought hope, but it was never suspected that he could win, that he could stop a foe that "dressed" so well for war:

the Yankee did not expect what was happening:
he dressed very well for war
shining shoes and weapons.

("That Friend," X)

Sandino's guerrillas "came forth / even from the whiskey that
was opened." It was a bloody confrontation which Sandino
won. "That Friend" is a powerful poem that evokes the daring
of great fighters. The West Point fighters came armed with
"learned" tactics. They had no field experience. They had
new technological weapons and expensive uniforms but no
experience and no understanding of the passion that inspired
Sandino and his men to fight:

the North Americans did not learn
that we love our sad beloved land
and that we will defend the flags
that with pain and love were created.
If they did not learn this in Philadelphia
they found it out through blood in Nicaragua:
the captain of the people waited there:
Augusto C. Sandino he was called.

("That Friend," X)

Neruda told it so that the historical account could be cleared.
He wanted the world to know that there were men who felt
capable of confronting and defeating the rule of the dollar.

But the tyrant against independent Latin American
governments was powerful, rich and very deceptive:

For peace, on a sad night
General Sandino was invited
to dine, to celebrate his courage,
with the "American" Ambassador
(for the name of the whole continent
the pirates have usurped.)
General Sandino was joyous:
wine and drinks raised to his health:

16

the Yankees were returning to their land
desolately defeated
and the banquet sealed with honors
the struggle of Sandino and his brothers.
The assassin waited at the table.
He was a mysterious spineless being
raising his cup time and again
while in his pocket resounded
the thirty horrendous dollars of the crime.

("Treason," XI)

Sandino was only one of the many fighting rulers who had
been assassinated as they strove to govern without
interference:

Sandino stood up not knowing
that his victory had ended
as the Ambassador pointed him out
thus fulfilling his part of the pact:
everything was arranged for the crime
between the assassin and the North American.
And at the door as they embraced him
they bade him farewell condemning him.
Congratulations! And Sandino took his leave
walking with the executioner and death.

("Death," XII)

The work of one man can be stopped only if his action
is not rooted in a public movement. Sandino's work was
interrupted but not stopped. However, Nicaragua saw a
powerful and long-lasting dictatorship assume power:

The killer of Sandino belonged to the "guardia nacional,"
a constabulary created by the United States to keep
order after the marines had left. The leader of this
force was a tough little warrior named Anastasio Somoza
but familiarly called "Tacho." Somoza was also the nephew
of President Sacasa, during whose administrations he

17

acquired a strong grip on the mechanisms of power. Soon he was announcing his advent to the presidency, implying that no one had better try to stop him. No one did. Somoza was the sole candidate in 1936, and he remained in power until he was assassinated twenty years later.
(John Edwin Fagg, *Latin America, A General History,* New York, 1969. See "The Traitor Dies," XIII.)

Somoza's assassination did not eliminate his influence from government. On the contrary, it was as if when Rigoberto Lopez killed Somoza, a plague had been released over all of Nicaragua:

> But from the guts that spilled
> came little Somozas:
> two clowns splattered with blood:
> from the cruel frog two little fertile frogs.
> Scarcely had the purulent one decayed,
> the two toy generals ascended,
> they embroidered themselves with diamonds
> became lifetime presidents
> dividing all of the haciendas between themselves
> they posed as the *nouveaux riches*
> making themselves the favorite warriors
> of the North American Ambassador.
> That is how history is made in our land:
> thus crimes are perpetuated:
> and the chain of the infamous persists
> in a cesspool of military tortures.
>
> ("Monarchs," XIV)

This tale of United States intervention in the national affairs of Latin American nations holds for the whole of the continent. It is a story full of violent aggression and deceptions. Neruda relates how he "saw the rose [of resistance] bloom in Guatemala" but that Guatemala "was assassinated / in full flight, like a dove" ("In Guatemala," XVI). He also depicts the brutal spilling of blood in El

Salvador, where "a bloody flavor soaks / the land, the bread and wine" ("In Salvador, Death," XVII).

The past when brought into the present arouses feelings of anger if what is being portrayed is a tale of tyranny and humiliation. It is clear to me that a Venezuelan reading the historical account that Neruda presents in poems XXIII to XXVI would find himself aroused to a pitch of anxiety. The events are so boldly stated and so passionately portrayed that I can see how a young Venezuelan reading a poem like "The Tiger" to his family might encounter the same crisis that I found myself in when I first read "Muñoz Marín" to my Uncle Al:

> Gómez was the name of that death.
> In half an hour he auctioned the petroleum
> to delinquent North Americans . . .
> fervent Venezuela bled.
> Gabaldón told me how from his cell
> he heard his comrade cry,
> he did not know what was happening
> until those short, cruel screams
> ended. And that was Venezuela's
> silence: no one answered.
> The worms and death lived.
> ("The Tiger," XXIV)

It is Neruda's personal contact with the history of Latin America that matters here. His involvement in the action is what makes him a purifier of the distorted historical record. To have a clear historical perspective the poet had had to be in touch with the men who risked their lives. It is because of Neruda's direct involvement that the poems are such powerful indictments against the events that unfurled:

> but Pérez Jiménez buried
> Venezuela and tormented her.
> Her stores were filled with pain,

> torn limbs and broken bones
> and the prisons once again were
> populated with the most honest men.
> ("Pérez Jiménez," XXV)

Honest men in jail. Thieves on the streets adorning themselves with the public's trust. Yet even when armed insurrection managed to topple these treacherous leaders, even when "the walls of the tyrant were broken / and the people unfettered their majesty," these defeated rulers found a "palace" in the "Free World" which awaited them with open arms (see "Pérez Jiménez," XXV).

Neruda perceived with clarity that the ruling class of Latin Americans was inexorably subservient to foreign interests. Rómulo Betancourt, Neruda informs us, was first an opportunist with foreign economic allegiances, and then secondly the President of Venezuela:

> Recommended by Muñoz Marín,
> at last they certified him in New York
> with titles of specialist in law and order,
> the gringos studied him a moment
> and deposited him in Caracas,
> wrapped up in their perspective:
> he learned English in order to obey orders,
> he was prompt and circumspect in everything:
> eyes and ears toward North America
> while to Venezuela deaf and blind.
> ("A Strange Democrat," XXVI)

Information about the past without an active memory to bring historical details into the present is static information that does not service people. Neruda understood that it is one of the primary responsibilities of the poet to be the living, accurate memory of his people.

20

II IMMEDIACY

When I am told a lie that is believed by the people I live
with but not by me, I am alone. I remember sitting in a barber
shop when the news of President Kennedy's death came over
the radio. The President of the United States had been shot
and it was only a matter of hours before the media was
flooded with assurances to the public that there had been no
conspiracy, that it was the act of only one man, one solitary
force carrying out its will without a "plot." I saw that the
public wanted to believe that there had been no larger context
for Oswald's action other than his own "nuttiness." I then saw
the televised assassination of Lee Harvey Oswald. It too was
believed to be the act of a solitary will doing its own most
powerful bidding. Jack Ruby shortly thereafter died of cancer.
No context. No conspiracy. Just individual men doing their
thing. I did not believe it. But the people I loved and trusted
believed it and that made me feel frustrated and anxious.

What do I do when I am told a lie about events that
have happened in my lifetime? I listen for stories. I do
not enter disputes on President Kennedy's murder. I do what
Neruda taught me to do. I just let information cruise in from
wherever it is coming and I then work at making a memory of
the stories that are clear to me. Fidel Castro is a clear story;
thus Neruda believed and celebrated Castro's work:

> But when torture and darkness
> seem to extinguish the free air
> and it is not the spume of the waves
> but the blood among the reefs that you see,
> Fidel's hand comes forth and in it
> Cuba, the pure rose of the Caribbean.
> And so History teaches with her light
> that man can change that which exists
> and if he takes purity into battle
> in his honor blooms a noble spring.
>
> ("Cuba Appears," IV)

21

The "tortures" are the lies, the distortion of events. The "darkness" is the fear that is experienced when there is no clarity, no story to believe. There are men who can deal with such times because they "can change that which exists." Neruda saw in Fidel Castro the "purity" of a self that put into action what he saw had to be done:

> Fidel Castro with fifteen of his men
> and liberty touched down on the sand.
> ("The Challenge," V)

It was a simple and humble beginning. Fidel Castro began to create his Cuba with a "handful of men on the sand."

The war waged on Fidel Castro once it was clear that he was going to retain his right to rule independent of the dollar is just now becoming current "news" in the serious journals of our nation. The story as told by Taylor Branch and George Crile III in *Harper's* is a story that lays out events that were up to now thought of only as the nightmare dreams of schizophrenic left-wing propagandists and revolutionaries:

> During the last days of the Eisenhower
> Administration the assassination of Fidel Castro presented
> itself as an engaging possibility to various people in
> Washington who had reason to mistrust a successful
> revolution so close to the coast of Florida. Some of these
> people discussed the possibility with the CIA, which had
> arranged sudden changes of government in Guatemala and
> Iran, and it has been said that a few agents left for the
> Caribbean with instructions to bring about a coup d' etat.
> Little more was heard from them until the debacle at the
> Bay of Pigs.
> (Editors' Introduction to Taylor Branch and George Crile
> III, "The Kennedy Vendetta: How the CIA waged a silent
> war against Cuba," *Harper's,* August, 1975.)

Neruda knew who Eisenhower was and he made it plain to the world that Eisenhower's duplicity was a bitter cruelty:

22

> My theme is about a ship that came
> filled with ammunition and happiness:
> its cargo exploded in La Habana,
> its agony was an ocean on fire.
> There were two Eisenhowers in partnership,
> one navigated under water
> and the other smiled in Argentina,
> one deposited the explosive,
> the other knighted the approaching men,
> one pushed the torpedo button
> the other lied to all America,
> one swam like a green octopus
> and the other was milder than an aunt.
> ("The Explosion of 'La Coubre' 1960" XXXI)

The problem of dealing with the immediate present is that accurate information about it is often not what the public believes. The crisis occurs when I cannot believe public information and I am left with feelings of loneliness and wrongdoing. That is why I look for people to believe with me what the majority of people do not. It is an isolated position that makes me vulnerable because it makes me fear. I live aware that there is no "safety," and that the environment I exist in is in crisis. Neruda insists on pointing out the crisis because it is the antidote to sleep. It never matters how deep the sleep has been. What matters is the awakening of consciousness as the individual deals with what is happening.

Neruda saw Castro as the antidote to Cuba's sleep. He perceived the deliberate web of lies that was spun around Castro as he worked to put his words into action:

> Fidel, Fidel, the people are grateful
> for words in action and deeds that sing.
> ("To Fidel Castro," XIX)

"Words in action" is the key to Neruda's perception. A man

who carries out his word is a man who makes himself concrete. Fidel was doing in Cuba what he "said" he would do, and that was surprising to those who thought that they could engage his services once he acquired power. The test of wills was on. Fidel Castro was confronted by the fears of weak Latin American leaders and President Kennedy's personal humiliation over the disaster of the Bay of Pigs:

> In Washington, President Kennedy struggled to comprehend how so total a disaster could have been produced by so many people who were supposed to know what they were doing, who had wrecked governments other than Castro's without mishap or detection. They had promised him a secret success but delivered a public fiasco. Communist rule in Cuba was to have been overthrown and Fidel Castro executed by Cuban citizens, all without evidence of American involvement; instead, Castro was heaping scorn on the "imperialist worms" he had defeated. Not only was the invasion an abject military failure, but the highest officials of the U. S. government were being subjected to worldwide ridicule for having tried to pass it off as the work of independent Cubans. The CIA's elaborate "cover story" had fallen into absurdity, and the President finally ended the charade by issuing a statement in which he assumed full responsibility for the invasion. With this admission, the Bay of Pigs became a virtual synonym for international humiliation, as well as the most egregious display of official American lying yet entered into the public record.
>
> (Branch and Crile, *op. cit.*)

Inside the United States the crisis "let loose the fear of war and rallied public opinion to the President's support." I did not rally around our President. But many friends of mine, including members of my family, began to deride Castro as an enemy. I saw the public animosity that grew as our media and statesmen came out against Castro. Neruda met their assertions with his story:

> It seems that nowadays
> lies gather against Cuba
> the wire dispatches them day and night
> preparing for the moment of attack:
> "It seems that the church is distrustful"
> "There is discontent in Cayo Benito"
> "Fidel did not show on the 28th"
>   ("The Ambush," XXI)

Neruda saw the "ambush" that awaited Castro and he also saw how Castro survived the lies while:

> meeting with other "latinos"
> equally sold out and perverse
> who yarn the lies of hell
> against Cuba each day:
> they alone concoct this stew.
>   ("The Ambush," XXI)

It is now public knowledge that costly plots and military action against Castro were paid for and run by CIA agents. Yet Castro survived the rich and international power of the CIA. This is a deed that no other Latin American revolutionary leader has accomplished. Fidel Castro has weathered the severest storm of technological sabotage and espionage waged by the CIA in the Caribbean. Castro's crisis and the war that he is winning against the CIA have made clear to the world that with determination a rich enemy can be stopped and his lies can be exposed. Our present investigations of CIA covert activities inside our national borders testify to the tyrannous power that this agency has acquired.

But as Castro carries out his word and people come to believe in how he works, a collective story in which to believe will grow in Cuba. In the immediate present, however, Castro faces the crisis of having to deal with the confusion of deliberately spun lies and attacks against Cuba that are financed by millions of dollars on an international scale by the

CIA. Neruda had seen what was happening. He also knew
that Castro would need a troubadour, a man who would sing
the deeds that he performed. Neruda assigned himself the
task of being that storyteller:

> I was born to sing these sorrows
> to expose destructive beasts . . .
> I stir up the grief of my people,
> I incite the root of their swords,
> I caress the memory of their heroes,
> I water their subterranean hopes,
> for to what purpose my songs,
> the natural gift of beauty and words,
> if it does not serve my people
> to struggle and walk with me?
> ("I Come from the South," XV)

III   ACTION

Neruda took his information right out of his experience
and he got his energy replenished by being with people:

> I am the man of bread and fish
> and you will not find me among books,
> but with women and men:
> they have taught me the infinite.
> ("So Is My Life," XXII)

People are the subject matter of these poems. The intention of
the book is to "attend to the pain / of those who suffer: they
are my pains" (XXII). Neruda sees it as his duty to assign
himself the task of recorder. No outside force could have made
him write these poems. It is an internal need to inform that is
at work. Neruda set out to create a "historical flow" that
would counter the "official" ignorance in which street people
are kept:

26

> Some people ask me that human affairs
> with names, surnames and laments
> not be dealt with in the pages of my books,
> not to give them space in my verses:
> they say poetry died here,
> some say I should not do it:
> the truth is I do not want to please them.
> ("Do Not Ask Me," XXIX)

Assigning the self a task to carry out is an effort toward balance and a grasp at sanity. When Neruda can believe in nothing, he gives himself something to do and he labors to make it through his self-assigned task:

> And so, if when I attack what I hate,
> or when I sing to those I love,
> poetry wants to abandon
> the hopes of my manifesto,
> I'll follow the letter of my law . . .
> ("Do Not Ask Me," XXIX)

The "letter" of Neruda's law is to move the potential power of the memory into action. Neruda works to bring the past into the now so that people can pay attention to the place that they are inhabiting:

> If you did not see the crimson of the "corocoro"
> flying like a suspended hive
> cutting the air like a scythe,
> the whole sky beating in flight
> as the scarlet plumage passes
> leaving a burning lightning bolt,
> if you did not see the Caribbean air
> flowing with blood without being wounded,
> you do not know the beauty of this world,
> you are not aware of the world you've lived in.
> ("Caribbean Birds," XXVII)

The poet pays attention to the immediate environment, to the geography of the nation, to the beauty of the land. Neruda creates powerful images in order to bring geographical sight to people:

> Panama, your geography granted you
> a gift that no other land was given:
> two oceans pushed forward to meet you:
> the cordillera tapered naturally:
> instead of one ocean it gave you the water
> of the two sovereigns of the foam,
> the Atlantic kisses you with lips
> that habitually kiss the grapes,
> while the Pacific Ocean shakes
> in your honor its cyclonic stature.
> ("History of a Canal," XXXIII)

Neruda balances his beautiful geographical descriptions with an equally accurate reminder of the economic crime that is being committed against the land:

> but men from other parts
> brought to you their yoke
> and they spilled nothing but whiskey
> since they mortgaged your waistline:
> and everything follows as it was planned
> by devils and their lies:
> with their money they built the Canal,
> they dug the earth with your blood
> and now dollars are sent to New York
> leaving you the graves.
> ("History of a Canal," XXXIII)

Neruda's perception tuned itself into the crisis of the moment. His task was to create images that would make the moment so rich with memories that he and people along with him would flow into action.

Many of the poems in *Song of Protest* create geographical images that describe and celebrate the natural beauty of the continent. Neruda was seeking a balance between giving people a memory and describing for them the natural riches that they actually live in. Both faculties are needed to have a grasp of what is happening. A man needs a memory and a live relationship with the land in order to develop independent muscles:

> like Panamanian wind asks
> like a child that has lost its mother
> where is the flag of my country?
> ("History of a Canal," XXXIII)

Neruda inspires personal action. The poems do not present a theory or a plan toward a revolution. Instead, Neruda creates historical and geographical pictures that stimulate the mind of the reader into the real. His action is to deliver a geographical-historical charge into his reader's muscle. In "The Heroes" Neruda swiftly sketches the fate of the men and women who have risked putting their muscles into action:

> But the students who shoot
> against evil, alone or scattered,
> will find no asylum in Embassies
> nor will they find ships in port
> nor planes to transport them to another place
> unless it is to where torments await them.
> They will be denied a visa to New York
> until the young clandestine hero
> is, later, denounced and discovered:
> they will leave no eyes in sockets,
> one by one they will crush the bones.
> Later they will show off at the UN
> in this Free World of ours,
> while the North American Minister
> gives Trujillo new weapons.
> This tale is terrible, and if you have suffered
> you will forgive me, I do not lament it.
> That is how the wicked perpetuate themselves:

29

this is reality and I do not lie.
("The Heroes," XXXVIII)

War is not the only road to a balance, and Neruda
makes it clear in "North American Friend" that he can
see that there is hope for mutual understanding with the
northern "workers broad, narrow and bent / over wheels and
flames." Neruda does not visualize the north as only a place
full of monsters and liars. He asserts that he wants to share
learning but he finds that

> ...Two or three people
> close the North American doors
> and only the "Voice of America" is heard
> which is like listening to a lean chicken.
> ("North American Friend," XXXIX)

In the United States we ourselves have been satiated
with "listening" to the "lean chicken" broadcasts that carry
the lies of our national government around the world. We
have just been discovering the need to expose the deceptions
that the highest officers of our land release to us through an
incessant media that carries public announcements of
falsehood into the most private spaces of our lives. The media
could be a positive instrument for shaping future time, but for
now it pecks at our lives with its endless attacks on our senses
as it sells us merchandise that in the getting depletes the
world's natural resources. Neruda sees through to this
nation's greed when he speaks his balanced vision:

> We are not going to exploit your petroleum,
> we will not intervene with customs,
> we will not sell electrical energy
> to North American villages:
> we are peaceful people who can
> be content with the little we earn,
> we do not want to submit anyone

30

> to coveting the circumstances of others.
> We respect Lincoln's space
> and Paul Robeson's clear conscience.
> We learned to love Charlie Chaplin
> (although his power was evilly rewarded).
> And so many things, the geography
> that unites us in the desired land,
> everything tells me to say once again
> that we are sailing in the same boat:
> it could sink with pride:
> let us load it with bread and apples,
> let us load it with Blacks and Whites,
> with understanding and hopes.
>
> (North American Friend," XXXIX)

Neruda proposes a vision of unity that we have not yet achieved inside the national borders of the United States. We are not going to find unity with Latin America either until we settle the domestic problem of public lies told us in the name of "National Security." Neruda does not conceive a need to come north to destroy or to be revenged. He simply teaches the expulsion of the dollar and the moral and economic manipulation that it imposes wherever it flourishes.

Neruda's final gesture in *Song of Protest* is to sing a song of praise. He sings the praise of the Sierra Maestra whose rugged landscape had long offered a home to Cuban patriots. Neruda celebrates "the rough groves, / the tough habitat of the rocks" because he knew the risk that Castro was taking as he made himself a coherent story for the Cuban people to believe in. Castro's remarkable administration "had not lost its puritanical character, and it was probably the least corrupt that Cuba had known for decades." (John Edwin Fagg, *Latin America, A General History* [New York, 1969], p. 580.) Neruda felt deep trust in the purity of Castro's intention. He saw in Fidel a warrior who had the fire to purify the present and to create a future where clarity would prevail:

I see what's coming and what's being born,
the pains that were defeated,
the destitute hopes of my people:
the children in school with shoes,
the giving out of bread and justice
as the sun gives out with summer.
I see fulfilled simplicity . . .
                    ("Written in the Year 2000," XLII)

In his meditation over the Sierra Maestra, Neruda projects his vision into future time as he perceives a world of working men where "there is no necessity to run / between governors and courts of justice" because it is a world in which "the cruel and the bad are gone forever." "Written in the Year 2000" is Neruda's vantage point from which he asserts:

In this space the turbulent weight
of my life neither overcomes nor weeps,
I discharge the pain that visits me
as I release a pigeon:
if there is accounting to be done, it must be done
with what's to come and what's beginning,
with the happiness of all the world
and not with what time crumbles.
                    ("Written in the Year 2000," XLII)

His meditation points the way to the joy of work. Each man delights in "what's to come" if he is the maker of it. Neruda asks that we look at "what's beginning." He shows that the action of one man never ends because "another takes mysterious arms: / human rebirth has no end . . ." In the last poem of *Song of Protest* (XLIII), Neruda announces a "Final Judgment" that he did not write because men of action are now just acquiring their independent muscles. Neruda leaves their fate on the heights of the Sierra Maestra to grow strong in their battle:

I leave it on this summit protected,
high, undulating over the prairies,
representing for the oppressed peoples
the dignity born out of fighting . . .
  ("Written in the Year 2000," XLII)

PREFACE

At first I centered this book around Puerto Rico, its tormented colonial condition, the actual struggle of its insurgent patriots.

The book later grew with the magnanimous events in Cuba and it developed in the Caribbean area.

I therefore dedicate it to the liberators of Cuba: Fidel Castro, his comrades and the Cuban people.

I dedicate it to those in Puerto Rico and in all of the vocal Caribbean world who fight for liberty and truth always threatened by the United States of North America.

This book is not a solitary lament or an emanation from darkness, but rather a direct and aimed weapon, an elemental and fraternal aid that I render to sibling nations in their daily struggle.

Those who before reproached me to excess will continue to reproach me more. For my part I here assume once again, with pride, my duties as poet of public utility, that is to say a pure poet. Poetry has always had the purity of water or of fire which cleans or burns without doubt.

I would hope that my poetry serves my brethren in the Caribbean as implements of honor. There is much to wash and burn all over America.

Much must be constructed.

May everyone arrive at what is his with sacrifice and happiness.

Our nations have suffered so much that we will have given them little when we have given them everything.

Pablo Neruda

Aboard the freighter *Louis Lumière* between America and Europe, April 12, 1960.

AUTHOR'S PREFACE IN 1968 FOR
THE THIRD URUGUAYAN EDITION

It is known that I wrote this book in 1960. Since then I have traveled the Americas reading it to large and small audiences. In my country I have read its songs in praise of the Cuban Protest from the northern desert to beyond the Strait of Magellan. Mexico and Peru heard these verses. Students and workers were the majority of my fervent public. When invited by the P.E.N. Club in the United States to one of its conventions, I read my lyric, epic and anti-imperialist poetry before many large audiences in New York and California.

Some literary Cubans drafted and disseminated a letter against me that will pass into the modern history of infamy. Printed in Madrid, in printshops authorized by Franco, with the postal image of the fascist dictator, it was distributed by the thousands in Latin America. It was also given a costly and enormous distribution in Europe and Asia.

Song of Protest is still ardently alive in its numerous editions. It was the first book that any poet—in Cuba or anywhere else—had dedicated to the Cuban Revolution.

In authorizing this new Uruguayan edition of my book, I believe that those who will read these poems in the years to come will judge our era and that they will arrive at their own judgment of the lives and acts of one another.

Meanwhile my passion and my work will continue, as in this book, to fortify and defend the Cuban Revolution in spite of literary Cains. It is great historic acts that have importance in our peoples' journey, and history will disregard the offended and the offenses.

I swear, therefore, that my poetry will serve and sing of dignity to the indignant, of hope to the hopeless, of justice in spite of the unjust, of equality in spite of exploiters, of truth in spite of liars and of the great brotherhood of true fighters.

Pablo Neruda

Isla Negra, 1968.

I

Puerto Rico, Puerto Pobre

It is late, at this stage, for a beginning,
nevertheless this is my feeling:
here as in other times I come forth
to sing or to die: here I begin.
And there is no power that can silence me
except the sad magnitude of time
and of its ally: death with its plow
for the farming of bones.
I have chosen a theme hot
with blood, with palm trees and silence,
it is about an island surrounded
by many waters and infinite death:
there the pain of those who wait grows
and a river of lamentation bleeds,
it is a poor and incarcerated island,
ash-colored days come and go,
the light flies off and returns to the palms,
the night travels in its black ship
and there she is, there is the prisoner,
the island surrounded by suffering.
And our blood bleeds into hers
because a golden claw separates her
from her lovers and her birthright.

II

Muñoz Marín

There is a fat worm in these waters
in these lands a predatory worm:
he ate the island's flag
hoisting up his overseer's banner,
he was nourished from the captive blood
of the poor buried patriots.
On the golden crown of American wheat
the worm grew fat in a maggot heap
prospering in the monied shade,
bloodied with tortures and soldiers,
inaugurating false monuments,
making the native soil inherited
by their fathers an enslaved clod,
making an island as transparent as a star
into a small grave for slaves,
and this tapeworm lived among the poets,
by their own exile defeated,
he portioned out esteem to his teachers
paying pythagorean Peruvians
to propagate his government,
and his palace was white outside
and inside it was infernal like Chicago
with the mustache, the heart, the claws
of that traitor, of Luis Muñoz[1] the worm,
Muñoz Marín to the people,
Judas of the blood-let land,
overseer of the enslavement of the island,
corrupter of his poor brothers,
bilingual translator for the executioners,
chauffeur of North American whiskey.

40

III

It Is Happening

It is gay the arrow of these years
and our offended America is sad:
man climbs toward space on his satellite
and on the moon he nails his spikes,
meanwhile Nicaragua rots
in a dynasty of worms
dishonoring Sandino's[2] blood
and Rubén Darío's[3] seed:
O Nicaragua, heart of the swan,
lineage of the enraged rapier,
lift the voice in your breast,
and the enraged sword of your life
and cut in blood and fire the manacles
that crown your lineage with thorns.
And that is how the emerald is looked on,
the waistline, the Indian coast
of small and slender America,
right up to the diamond green of the islands,
there looms a bloodied, poor land
it is half of a radiant island:
Trujillo's[4] teeth gnawed her
wound for thirty consecutive years
and one has neither peace nor moon,
no shadow, sun, only misfortune,
for when gunfire
from man destroyed wonder
and perhaps finally all existence
of kings, star-filled and exquisite,

like a spiderweb of pain
anger persists in the Americas,
the wrath of the poor and naked
the calamity of the tyrant and his covetousness,
meanwhile Muñoz of Puerto Pobre
falsifies his island's signature
and under the pirate's banner
he sells out language and reason, lands and delights,
sells our poor America's honor,
sells parents and grandparents and ashes.

IV

Cuba Appears

But when tortures and darkness
seem to extinguish the free air
and it is not the spume of the waves
but the blood among the reefs that you see,
Fidel's hand comes forth and in it
Cuba, the pure rose of the Caribbean.
And so History teaches with her light
that man can change that which exists
and if he takes purity into battle
in his honor blooms a noble spring:
behind is left the tyrant's night,
his cruelty and his insensible eyes,
the gold snatched by his claws,
his mercenaries, his cannibal judges,
his high monuments sustained
by torment, dishonor and crime:
everything falls in the dust of the dead
when the people set their violins
and looking forward interrupt and sing,
interrupt the hatred of shadows and watchdogs,
sing and wake the stars with their song
and pierce the darkness with guns.
And so Fidel came forth cutting shadows
so that the jasmine tree could dawn.

V

The Challenge

If the deep sea hushed its pains,
the earth lifted up hopes
that went ashore on the coast:
it was the arms and fists of the struggle:
Fidel Castro with fifteen of his men
and liberty touched down on the sand.
The island was dark like mourning,
but they raised a banner of light,
they had no weapons other than the dawn
and she still slept beneath the earth:
then they started in silence
the struggle and the path toward the stars.
Fatigued and fervent they walked
for honor and duty toward war
they had no weapons other than their blood:
they were naked as though in birth.
And thus was Cuba's liberty born
from that handful of men on the sand.
Then the dignity of naked men
dressed them with clothes from the mountain,
nourished them on unknown bread,
armed them with secret gunpowder,
those asleep awakened with them,
festering offenses emerged from the grave,
mothers sent their children off,
the peasant told of his sorrow,
and the pure army of the poor
grew and grew like the full moon:

it lost no soldiers in battle:
the cane field thrived in the storm:
the enemy left their weapons
abandoned on the roads:
the executioners trembled and fell,
stripped by the springtime,
with a death-shot, the final
decorations pinned to their shirts,
while the movement of free people
moved, like the wind, the prairies,
shook the furrows of the island,
came forth over the sea like a planet.

VI

Ancient History

Now I open my eyes and I remember:
it sparkles and dims, electric and dark,
with joys and suffering
the bitter and magic history of Cuba.
Years passed as fish pass
through the blue of the sea and its sweetness,
the island lived in liberty and dance,
the palm trees danced with the foam,
Blacks and Whites were a single loaf of bread
because Martí[5] kneaded their ferment,
peace fulfilled its destiny of gold
and the sun crackled in the sugar,
while ripened by the sun fell
a beam of honey over the fruit:
man was content with his reign
and family with its agriculture,
when from the North arrived a seed
threatening, covetous, unjust,
that like a spider spread her threads
extending a metallic structure
that drove bloodied nails into the land
raising over the dead a vault.
It was the dollar with its yellow teeth,
commandant of blood and grave.

VII

Mid-Land

The Americas shape their waist
where the two oceans marry,
from the Atlantic they gather foam,
from the Pacific torrents of stars,
vessels from the white poles come
filled with petroleum and orange blossoms:
the seagoing warehouses sucked in
our secret mineral blood
that builds the skyscrapers on the planet
in cruel and thorny cities.
And so the empire of the dollar
became rooted there with its attending demons:
the bloodied Caribbean cannibals
disguised as heroic generals:
a leadership of pitiless mice,
an inheritance of armed spit,
a stinking cavern of imperious orders,
a gutter of tropical mud,
a black chain of torments,
a rosary of unsurpassed misery
while the dollar steers immorality
with a white fleet over the seas,
extracting the aroma of the plantain,
the hard grain of the coffee fields,

perpetuating in our pure land
the bloodstained Trujillos.
Poor America up to her waist
in blood in her many slums,
crucified on a cross with thorns,
handcuffed and gnawed by dogs,
torn into pieces by the invaders,
wounded by aggression and calamity,
razed by false winds,
sacrilegious wholesale and gigantic plundering.
O lean chain of sorrows,
O gathering place for the tears of two oceans.

VIII

Also in the Distant South

Thus the flowering hearts of our republics
have been bled in penitentiaries:
Cuba's heart was wrung
by Batista's[6] executioners
though before, Ubico[7] had imposed on Guatemala
a tragic iron lock of greed.
In the widest lands of the planet,
mountains or yellow Patagonian wastes,
volcanoes crowned with snow,
equatorial rivers beating,
in the Amazonic South of America,
the scars of tyranny
mar the broken fortresses of Paraguay
and the bitter stones of Bolivia.

IX

I Remember a Man

As I speak of the torrid palm trees
that the Caribbean kisses and shakes
I'll say that among many black eyes
those of Martí were the most courageous.
That man saw near and far
and now his eyes sparkle
as if time could not arrest their energy:
it is the eyes of Cuba that come to birth.
And then it was hard and dark work
to lift an independent laurel:
to dream of liberty was danger,
it meant changing life for death:
but Martí with hope and gunfire
awakened the daydreamer and the peasant
building with blood and thought
the architecture of the new light.

X

That Friend

Later Sandino crossed the jungle,
he unloaded his sacred gunpowder
against assaulting sailors
grown and paid for in New York:
the earth burned, the foliage resounded:
the Yankee did not expect what was happening:
he dressed very well for war
shining shoes and weapons
but through experience he soon learned
who Sandino and Nicaragua were:
it was a tomb of blond thieves:
air, tree, road, water
Sandino's guerrillas came forth
even from the whiskey that was opened,
which sickened with quick death
the glorious Louisiana fighters
accustomed to hanging blacks
with superhuman valor:
two thousand hooded men busy
with one black man, a rope and a tree.
Affairs were different here:
Sandino attacked and waited,
Sandino was the coming night,
he was the light from the sea that killed.
Sandino was a tower with flags,
Sandino was a rifle with hopes.
These were very different lessons,
at West Point learning was clean:

they were never taught at school
that he who kills could also die:
the North Americans did not learn
that we love our sad beloved land
and that we will defend the flags
that with pain and love were created.
If they did not learn this in Philadelphia
they found it out through blood in Nicaragua:
the captain of the people waited there:
Augusto C. Sandino he was called.
And in this song his name will remain
full of wonder like a sudden blaze
so that it can give us light and fire
in the continuation of his battles.

XI

Treason

For peace, on a sad night
General Sandino was invited
to dine, to celebrate his courage,
with the "American" Ambassador
(for the name of the whole continent
these pirates have usurped).
General Sandino was joyous:
wine and drinks raised to his health:
the Yankees were returning to their land
desolately defeated
and the banquet sealed with honors
the struggle of Sandino and his brothers.
The assassin waited at the table.
He was a mysterious spineless being
raising his cup time and again
while in his pockets resounded
the thirty horrendous dollars of the crime.
O feast of bloodied wine!
O night, O false moonlit paths!
O pale stars that did not speak!
O land mute and blind by night!
Earth that did not restrain his horse!
O treasonous night that betrayed
the tower of honor into evil hands!
O banquet of silver and agony!
O shadow of premeditated treason!
O pavilion of light that flourished,
since then defeated and mourned!

XII

Death

Sandino stood up not knowing
that his victory had ended
as the Ambassador pointed him out
thus fulfilling his part of the pact:
everything was arranged for the crime
between the assassin and the North American.
And at the door as they embraced him
they bade him farewell condemning him.
Congratulations! And Sandino took his leave
walking with the executioner and death.

XIII

The Traitor Dies

Somoza[8] was the traitor's name
the mercenary, the tyrant, the executioner.
I have said his name was, because one day
a thunderbolt came to nail him to the wall.
Nicaragua knows sacrifices,
the imposed manipulation of her spirit
while her leaders wrote
with greedy potbellied pens and a mule's voice,
comparing him to God and to the planets,
to the rosy silver of dawn,
while he strangled Nicaragua
with a thief's hands and turbulent fingers.
Valiant Rigoberto Lopez came:
he found him rejoicing in his affairs
and he cut his life short with a burst
of rapid angry gunfire.
Thus fell the perforated abdomen
and dead honor was restored.
The hero who brought fire died there:
he shaped his destiny with his fists.
His heroic exploit was his seed of death!
May the universal hymn honor his name!

XIV

Monarchs

But from the guts that spilled
came little Somozas:
two clowns splattered with blood:
from the cruel frog two little fertile frogs.
Scarcely had the purulent one decayed,
the two toy generals ascended,
they embroidered themselves with diamonds
became lifetime presidents
dividing all haciendas between themselves,
they posed as *nouveaux riches*
making themselves the favorite warriors
of the North American Ambassador.
That is how history is made in our land:
thus crimes are perpetuated:
and the chain of the infamous persists
in a cesspool of military tortures.

XV

I Come from the South

I was born to sing these sorrows,
to expose destructive beasts,
to contain shamelessness with a scourge,
to touch inhuman scars.
I am of American parentage,
born from Araucanian[9] ashes,
for when the invader searched for gold
my country attacked him with fire and pain.
In other lands he dressed in gold:
here the conqueror did not conquer:
greedy Pedro de Valdivia[10]
found what he looked for in my country:
he died underneath a cinnamon tree
with molten gold in his throat.
I represent tribes that fell
defending their beloved banners
with nothing left but silence and rain
after the splendor of their battles,
but I continue their action
and throughout all of America
I stir up the grief of my people,
I incite the root of their swords,
I caress the memory of their heroes,
I water their subterranean hopes,
for to what purpose my songs,
the natural gift of beauty and words,
if it does not serve my people
to struggle and walk with me?
So I go throughout oppressed America
lighting fuses and lamps,

tyrants deny me a passport
because my poetry frightens them:
if they bolt the doors against me,
I come, like light, through windows,
if they ignite the territories against me
I enter by rivers flowing with water,
my poetry reaches into prisons
to converse with him who looks for me,
with the fugitive I count stars
all night, in the morning I part:
the ocean's reefs do not detain me:
machine guns do not stop me:
my poems are the eyes of dawn,
they're fists of stone and winged hearts.
When people recognize me on the street,
in copper or barley fields,
from trains that cross the countryside,
on bitter sweet plantations,
if greeted in remote ports
or in infernal subterranean mines
it is my poetry that has passed there
with its wheel of love and vengeance
to establish worldwide clarity
to give light to those who hope for it
to advance victory to those who struggle
to give the earth to those who work it.

In Guatemala

Just as in Sandino's time
I saw the rose bloom in Guatemala.
I saw the poor man's land defended,
and justice arrive to every mouth.
Arbenz[11] opened amidst his people
his delicate and powerful hand
and schools were a granary
of triumphant possibilities
till from the Canal long claws
severed the dawn's path.
The North American arsonists
dropped dollars and bombs:
death built its finery,
the United Fruit uncoiled its rope.
And thus Guatemala was assassinated
in full flight, like a dove.

In Salvador, Death

In Salvador, death still patrols.
The blood of dead peasants
has not dried, time does not dry it,
rain does not erase it from the roads.
Fifteen hundred were machine-gunned.
Martinez[12] was the assassin's name.
Since then a bloody flavor soaks
the land, the bread and wine in Salvador.

XVIII

Liberty

Caribbean treasures, luxurious foam
spilt over illustrious blues,
fragrant coasts of silver and gold
seeming, ornamented by sand,
intense archipelago of dreams,
boundaries of whispers and sudden blazes,
castles of floating palm trees,
pineapple perfumed mountains,
sonorous islands moving to the wind's
dance like invited brides,
races the color of night and wood,
eyes like starry nights,
statues that dance in the jungle
as the sea makes love to the waves,
saffron hips that sustain
the rhythm of love in the grove,
breasts dark as country smoke
with the odor of jasmine in huts,
heads united by sunset,
smiles nourished by the moon,
coconut trees yielding to the wind,
people as sonorous as guitars,
poverty of islands and coast,
men without land, children without spoons,
rhythmic young women moved
by a deep African drum,
dark heroes of the coffee fields,
hard workers of the cane,

children of the water, father of the sugar,
petroleum and banana athletes
O Caribbean of dazzling gifts,
O land and sea splattered with blood,
O Antilles destined for heaven,
by the Devil and men mistreated,
now the hour of hours has come:
the hour of the breaking dawn,
and whoever threatens to annihilate the light
will fall stripped of life:
and when I say that the hour has come
I think of freedom reconquered:
I think that in Cuba grows a seed
one thousand times itself loved and awaited:
the seed of our dignity,
for so long wounded and trod under heel,
falls in the furrow—thus the flags of the
American revolution are raised.

XIX

To Fidel Castro

Fidel, Fidel, the people are grateful
for words in action and deeds that sing,
that is why I bring from far
a cup of my country's wine:
it is the blood of a subterranean people
that from the shadows reaches your throat,
they are miners who have lived for centuries
extracting fire from the frozen land.
They go beneath the sea for coal
but on returning they are like ghosts:
they grew accustomed to eternal night,
the working-day light was robbed from them,
nevertheless here is the cup
of so much suffering and distances:
the happiness of imprisoned men
possessed by darkness and illusions
who from the inside of mines perceive
the arrival of spring and its fragrances
because they know that Man is struggling
to reach the amplest clarity.
And Cuba is seen by the southern miners,
the lonely sons of la pampa,
the shepherds of cold in Patagonia,
the fathers of tin and silver,
the ones who marry cordilleras
extract the copper from Chuquicamata,
men hidden in buses
in populations of pure nostalgia,

women of the fields and workshops,
children who cried away their childhoods:
this is the cup, take it, Fidel.
It is full of so much hope
that upon drinking you will know your victory
is like the aged wine of my country
made not by one man but by many men
and not by one grape but many plants:
it is not one drop but many rivers:
not one captain but many battles.
And they support you because you represent
the collective honor of our long struggle,
and if Cuba were to fall we would all fall,
and we would come to lift her,
and if she blooms with all her flowers
she will flourish with our own nectar.
And if they dare touch Cuba's
forehead, by your own hands liberated,
they will find the peoples' fists,
we will take out our buried weapons:
blood and pride will come to rescue,
to defend our beloved Cuba.

XX

Returning to Puerto Pobre

While laurels rise to Cuba's
victory, glistening throughout the universe,
an arrow pierces my soul
and my vigil returns to Puerto Rico.
And now that our peoples have sung
why suddenly was it like a wound,
this mortal chain of silence?
When liberty came to Cuba
flags trembled in the wind,
but a sister flag was missing:
your people's colors were missing.
When each nation sang its song
of victory and suffering
each national voice spoke its verse.
You lowered your eyes in silence.
Muñoz the Liar sent his acceptance
telegram tainted with fear,
but your voice was imprisoned,
your poor heart in jail.
The North American put down his foot
on Muñoz and dictated a decree
and under that decree and those feet
the Commonwealth stinks of death.
Associated Muñoz goes up and down
the corridors of the Administration

offering poor Puerto Rico
a coffin of bloody dollars.
O poor Puerto Rico Puerto Pobre
nailed by the nails of torment
by your treasonous sons who pierce
your bones on a cross of bloody dollars.
Nevertheless I announce your new day:
I announce the arrival of your time:
the mercenaries will roll in dust
and your suffering will be crowned,
dignity will be reestablished,
your own voice, your own thought:
you will expel Chicago's seal,
and your flag will swell in the wind.

XXI

The Ambush

It seems that nowadays
lies gather against Cuba
the wire dispatches them day and night
preparing for the moment of attack:
"It seems that the church is distrustful"
"There is discontent in Cayo Benito"
"Fidel did not show on the 28th"
"Vision" meets in its infamous office
its gang of renegades and ghouls,
Bolivians who lick each dollar
and who insult their poor birth,
crucifying Bolivia's hunger,
and auctioning off all our kingdom
meeting with other "latinos"
equally sold out and perverse
who yarn the lies of hell
against Cuba each day:
they alone concoct this stew.
In this restaurant they give no orders.
They only add sauce to calumny
and serve it: they're kitchen boys and busboys.
This dish is cooked far away
it contains bomb raids as well,
the massacre of children and women,
and another Batista, with a new name:
and nothing's happened here, is what they think.
"The rest we'll settle with money."
But this time they'll pay with blood.
And they will not conquer any except the dead.

XXII

So Is My Life

My duty moves along with my song:
I am I am not: that is my destiny.
I exist not if I do not attend to the pain
of those who suffer: they are my pains.
For I cannot be without existing for all,
for all who are silent and oppressed,
I come from the people and I sing for them:
my poetry is song and punishment.
I am told: you belong to darkness.
Perhaps, perhaps, but I walk toward the light.
I am the man of bread and fish
and you will not find me among books,
but with women and men:
they have taught me the infinite.

XXIII

For Venezuela

I loved Venezuela but she was not there.
I sought her among the names that lived:
I called and called, no one responded,
the submerged nation did not respond,
nevertheless the map conceded her
a geographic emerald,
the mountains with snow-white birds,
a blue fire protected the islands,
the petroleum burned her hips
and embroidered her lining with gold,
the Orinoco[13] was an infinite letter
written with caymans and news,
in fact, in fact, Venezuela sounded
like a hardware capital
with diamonds, peelings and tapirs
breathing with Simón Bolívar
(while a gentleman arrived in Chile
to madden us with his orthography).
And so I walked throughout the world,
I knocked on friendly and hostile doors
and all nations in their turn
arranged themselves for my visit
just as I had seen them on the map in childhood:
green Asia, carnivorous England,

Spain inaugurating its sepulchers,
fragrant France barely clothed,
Switzerland like a watch among madmen,
Germany practicing artillery,
Russia changed her name,
in Rome God lodged and suffered,
as I searched for Venezuela
and spent my days without finding her
till Picón Salas[14] de Caracas
came and explained to me what was happening.

XXIV

The Tiger

Gómez[15] was the name of emptiness
Gómez was the name of that death.
In half an hour he auctioned the petroleum
to delinquent North Americans
and since then he continued at his leisure.
And Venezuela silently
sank into the obscurity of prisons,
into the sickness of penitentiaries and fevers.
Those who were to be my brothers
walked through hostile roads
excavating rocks and carrying crickets:
fervent Venezuela bled.
Gabaldón[16] told me how from his cell
he heard a political prisoner die:
the worms ate him alive,
he heard his comrade cry,
he did not know what was happening
until those short, cruel screams
ended. And that was Venezuela's
silence: no one answered.
The worms and death lived.

XXV

Pérez Jiménez

Liberty with Medina Angarita[17]
decorum with Rómulo Gallegos[18]
they crossed Venezuela escaping
like birds in flight from other lands
and the beasts of terror returned
to raise their feet and hair.
The pregnant night gave birth to him:
Pérez Jiménez[19] was named the bat.
He was rotund of soul with a pestilent
belly, a thief and sly,
he was a fat lizard from the swamp
a gnawing monkey, an obese parrot,
he was a spineless mugger
a cross between a frog and a crab,
Trujillo's and Somoza's bastard
procreated in the State Department
for the internal use of monopolies,
for which he was a yellow doormat,
ambiguous by-product of petroleum
voracious shark of excrement.
This escaped frog from the swamp
dedicated himself to his own budget:
outside all ribbons and medals,
property and dollars inside,
he promoted to succulent ranks
his military courage without wars.
So much for the comedy I describe
in picturesque words,

but Pérez Jiménez buried
Venezuela and tormented her.
Her stores were filled with pain,
torn limbs and broken bones
and the prisons once again were
populated with the most honest men.
Thus the past returned to Venezuela
to lift its bloody whip
until throughout the streets of Caracas
horns united in the wind,
the walls of the tyrant were broken,
and the people unfettered their majesty.
The rest is once again new and ancient
the same sad history of our time:
the majestic tyrant toward Miami
ran like a somnambulist rabbit:
there he has a palace and the Free World
awaits him with open arms.

XXVI

A Strange Democrat

Betancourt[20] sat on Venezuela's
hopes like a heavy load,
this man is square outside
and opaque inside like cheese:
he prepared himself well for the Presidency
(but to be a man he never had time).
Recommended by Muñoz Marín,
at last they certified him in New York
with titles of specialist in law and order,
the gringos studied him for a moment
and deposited him in Caracas,
wrapped up in their perspective:
he learned English in order to obey orders,
he was prompt and circumspect in everything:
eyes and ears toward North America
while to Venezuela deaf and blind
he ordered from North American tailors
his pants and thoughts
until speaking with the Master's Voice
he forgot Venezuela and his people.
Cuba caused him strange annoyance,
because of Fidel he lost sleep,
all these reforms, giving land
to those who work it, what a bother!
and to give houses to all Cubans
is to convert Cuba into an inferno!
to sell sugar to those who buy it
is an intolerable impudence!

poor Betancourt was made
into a sorrowful Cain of our day.
Then in Caracas flourished
an insurrection of tender children:
the rebellious students
entrenched themselves in their discontent.
Betancourt, the warrior, instantly sent
his police and regiments,
his tanks, his planes, his guns,
he machine-gunned defenseless children,
and in front of schools in mourning
between the blackboards and notebooks
this "North American" democrat
left dozens of slaughtered young people.
Once again Venezuela covered with blood.
Herod Betancourt kept silent.

XXVII

Caribbean Birds

In this brief gust of wind without men
I invite you to celebrate birds,
the martin, swift sail of the wind,
the dazzling light of the hummingbird
housecleaner that divides the sky
for the gloomy crane
until the substance of dawn
weaves the color of the "aguaitacaminos."
O birds precious stones of the Caribbean,
quetzal, nuptial beam of Paradise,
air born jewelry of the foliage
birds of yellow lightning
kneaded with drops of turquoise
and the fire of naked catastrophes:
come to my small human song,
water troupial, simple partridge,
thrushes of miraculous forms,
earthbound "chocorocay,"
light dancers of gold and air,
spear-tailed ultraviolet "tintora,"
rock roosters, water birds,
companions, mysterious friends,
how did feathers surpass flowers?
Golden Mask, invincible woodpecker,
what can I do to sing in the midst
of Venezuela, next to your nests,

brilliant, celestial semaphore,
martins fishermen of dew
from the Far South my voice is
opaque, the voice of a somber heart,
am I nothing on Caribbean sand
but a rock that comes from the cold?
How am I to sing the melody,
the plumage, the light, the power
of what I saw without believing
or heard without believing I heard?
because the red heron went by me:
they were flying like a red river
against the Venezuelan brilliance,
the burning blue sun in sapphire
surged like an eclipse of beauty:
these birds flew from the ceremony itself.
If you did not see the crimson of the "corocoro"
flying like a suspended hive
cutting the air like a scythe,
the whole sky beating in flight
as the scarlet plumage passes
leaving a burning lightning bolt,
if you did not see the Caribbean air
flowing with blood without being wounded,
you do not know the beauty of this world,
you are not aware of the world you've lived in.

And that is why I speak and sing
and see and live for all men:
it is my duty to tell what you don't know
and what you do know I'll sing with you:
your eyes accompany my words
and my words flourish in the wheat
and they fly with the wings of the Caribbean
or they fight against your enemies.
I have so many duties, friends, that I am
moving on to another theme, so I take my leave.

XXVIII

Mean Events

If New York City shines like gold
and there are buildings with five hundred bars,
here I will write that they were made
with the sweat of the canefields:
the banana plantation is a green inferno
so that people may drink and dance in New York.
When at five thousand meters
the Chileans spit up blood
to export copper to New York
the Bolivians collapse with hunger
gouging the tin mines,
breaking the walls of the Andes,
and from the roots of the Orinoco
diamonds are scattered on the mud.
Through stolen Panamanian soil,
through stolen water, the ships go
to New York with our petroleum,
with our hijacked minerals
that with grave reverence our
decorated leaders hand over to them.
Sugar builds the walls,
Chilean nitrate the cities,
Brazilian coffee buys the beds,
Paraguay gives them universities,
from Colombia they receive emeralds,
while from Puerto Rico, that "associated"
island, the soldiers leave for their battle
(they fight in a singular manner
North Americans supply weapons
Puerto Ricans give their blood).

XXXIX

Do Not Ask Me

Some people ask me that human affairs
with names, surnames and laments
not be dealt with in the pages of my books,
not to give them space in my verses:
they say poetry died here,
some say I should not do it:
the truth is I do not want to please them.
I greet them, I tip my hat to them,
and I leave them voyaging in Parnassus
like happy rats in cheese.
I belong to another category,
I am only a man of flesh and bones,
therefore if they beat my brother
I defend him with what I have in hand
and each one of my lines carries
the threat of gunpowder or steel,
that will fall over the inhuman,
over the cruel and over the arrogant.
But the punishment of my furious peace
menaces neither the poor nor the good:
with my lamp I search for those who fall:
I soothe and close their wounds:
these are the chores of the poet
of the aviator and of the stonecutter:
we should do something on this earth
because we were born on this planet
and we must arrange man's society
because we are neither birds nor dogs.

And so, if when I attack what I hate,
or when I sing to those I love,
poetry wants to abandon
the hopes of my manifesto,
I'll follow the letter of my law
accumulating stars and armaments
and in my steadfast duty to America
one more rose does not matter:
I have a pact of love with beauty:
I have a pact of blood with my people.

XXX

OAS Meeting

Whether or not you are familiar with diplomacy
it is a matter that interests no one,
but this science has its twists
its frozen or infernal jungles
and today I must open the eyes of the just,
to teach what everyone already knows
and to demonstrate how far, uniting,
our nations could shake loose
and not be mere furniture
for Uncle Sam to sit on.
Our assembled ambassadors
form a soft silk cushion
and for that sacrosanct rump
Argentina designs its wool,
Ecuador its best macaw,
Peru its ancestral llamas,
Santo Domingo sends its nephews,
its brothers-in-law and other animals.
Chile is original like no other
and designates as representative
a bottle of wine without wine
or an inkwell without ink filled with vinegar.
And thus these gentlemen prepare
their long ineffable meetings,
they balance one on top of the other
with very interesting acrobatics
they fight to be the first cushion:
"At least they should step on me"

claims the delegate from Colombia
writing a sonnet, making the sign of the cross
while the delegate from Paraguay
with the one from Salvador, without clawing,
aspire to be the exclusive seats,
expressing their desire so obviously
that it moves everyone, but
just in time for the duel
their North American Chief arrives:
he sits on everyone without noticing
whom he sat upon first,
and an extravagant silence pervades.
The pressured Chief dictates accord
and returns to his important offices,
our Ambassadors regain composure,
they straighten their elegant jackets
and thus this meeting ends.
Gentlemen, the OAS has defects
but it is deliciously unanimous.

XXXI

The Explosion of "La Coubre" 1960[21]

My theme is about a ship that came
filled with ammunition and happiness:
its cargo exploded in La Habana,
its agony was an ocean on fire.
There were two Eisenhowers in partnership,
one navigated under water
and the other smiled in Argentina,
one deposited the explosive,
the other knighted the approaching men,
one pushed the torpedo button
the other lied to all America,
one swam like a green octopus
and the other was milder than an aunt.
These two parallel characters
learned that our geography
is controlled by rootless governments
that relinquished sovereignty:
for these leaders North America
is not always an empty cash box:
they give it all they have:
hopes and police
while premiere Eisenhower promenades
through palaces and avenues
without seeing a real person:
only ferocious office tigers
that want to sell him our flags.
But in the USA it was known
that with Fidel one speaks differently

and when in Cuba the peasants see
words of light for the first time
received in dignity
they have acquired books and land:
pale Eisenhower takes off
the half-mask of goodness
transforms himself into a frogman and swims
like a shark toward its prey.
Then the assassinated "La Coubre"
writhes between the wounded and embers:
they assassinate Frenchmen and Cubans
for the North American politicians
but the bandit submarines
have lost their grinding power
because they will not succeed in killing Cuba:
She will live, we swear it, this star:
we will fight for her revolution
until her last hand shoots
the last stone defending her honor.

XXXII

Americas

Viva Colombia beautiful and mournful,
and Ecuador crowned by fire,
viva small wounded Paraguay
resurrected by naked heroes,
O Venezuela you sing on the map
with the whole blue sky in motion
and I celebrate Bolivia's shy wilds,
her Indian eyes and light:
I know the common people fell
here and there defending our honor
and I love even the roots of my land
from the Rio Grande to the Chilean Pole
not only because in this long struggle
our bones are scattered,
but because I love each poor door
and each hand among these deep people
and there is no beauty like the beauty
of America stretched out in her infernos,
in her hills of rocks and power,
in her atavistic and eternal rivers,
I love you in the hidden spaces
of the cities smelling of dung,
in the trains of the vacillating daybreak,
in the markets, in the slaughterhouses,
in the electric flowers of Santos,
in the cruel design of your crabs,
in your decapitated miners,
and your turbulent drunkards:
the planet gave you all the snow,

large bodies of water and new volcanoes,
and then man went adding walls,
and inside of walls suffering
so it is for love that I beat your flanks:
receive me as if I were the wind.
I bring you a song that strikes
a love that cannot be content
and the fruitful bells:
the justice that our people yearn for.
It is not much to ask, we have so much,
nevertheless we have so little,
it is impossible that this continue.
This is my song, I ask this:
I ask nothing if not all,
I claim all for our people
and let him of sad ambition
be distracted by a title,
I continue and am assisted by two reasons:
my heart and my suffering.

XXXIII

History of a Canal

Panama, your geography granted you
a gift that no other land was given:
two oceans pushed forward to meet you:
the cordillera tapered naturally:
instead of one ocean it gave you the waters
of the two sovereigns of the foam,
the Atlantic kisses you with lips
that habitually kiss the grapes,
while the Pacific Ocean shakes
in your honor its cyclonic stature.
And so, small Panama, little sister,
I am now not taken by my first doubts,
I'll whisper them in your ear for I believe
that one must speak of bitterness in privacy.
And what happened? little sister, they cut
your figure as if it were cheese
and then ate and left you
like a gnawed olive pit.
I later found out the canal
was shaped like a moon river:
through that river the world was to arrive
spilling fortune on your sand,
but men from other parts
brought to you their yoke

and they spilled nothing but whiskey
since they mortgaged your waistline:
and everything follows as it was planned
by devils and their lies:
with their money they built the Canal,
they dug the earth with your blood
and now dollars are sent to New York
leaving you the graves.

XXXIV

Future of a Canal

Water passes through you like a knife
and separates love into two halves
with the chill of dollars stuck
up to the hilt in your honeycombs:
I tell you the sorrows that I feel;
if others do not see these calamities
you'll think that I am lost or that I drank
too many bottles in your bars:
but these constructions, these lakes,
these blue waters of two oceans
should not be the sword that divides
the miserable from the happy,
the door to this foam should be
the grand union of two nuptial oceans:
a small path constructed
for men and not exploiters,
for love not for money,
not for hate but for sustenance
and it must be said that to you belongs
this canal and all other canals
built on your territory:
these are your sacred springs.
The flow of the ocean that surrounds you
is yours, it is a vein for your blood,
and the vampires that devour it
should pack their valises and get out,
for only your sailing flag
should move in the afternoon wind:

the Panamanian wind asks
like a child that has lost its mother,
where is the flag of my country?
It is waiting. And Panama knows it.
And we Americans know it
from Patagonia to the Rio Grande:
only one flag in the Canal
should move its fragrant petal,
it cannot be a pirate flag
but yet another rose from our blood,
for Panama's national colors
will preside over the passage of ships.

XXXV

The Free "Press"

While briefly chilled, I want to tell
without vengeance and what's more with joy
how from my bed in Buenos Aires
the police took me to prison.
It was late, we had just arrived from Chile,
and without saying anything to us
they plundered my friend's papers,
they offended the house in which I slept.
My wife vented her disdain
but there were orders to be executed
and in a moving car we roved about
the tyrannous black night.
Then it was not Perón, [22] it was another,
a new tyrant for Argentina
and by his orders doors opened,
bolt after bolt was unlocked
in order to swallow me, the patios passed,
forty bars and the infirmary,
but still they took me up into a cell,
the most impenetrable and hidden:
only there did they feel protected
from the exhalations of my poetry.
I discovered through that broken night
that three thousand were imprisoned that day:
jail, penitentiary, and as if not enough,
boats were set adrift
filled with men and women,
the pride of Argentinean souls.

My tale comes only to this:
the rest is collective history:
I wanted to read it in newspapers,
in *La Prensa* (which is so informative),
yet Mr. Gaínza Paz[23] does not know
if Argentinean prisons are being filled.
He is the champion of our "free" press
but if communist journals are closed
this grandee acts dumb without reporting it,
his feet ache and he has eye trouble,
and if the workers go to jail
everybody knows it except Gaínza,
everybody resorts to newspapers,
but "large" journals do not publish
anything about these stupid tales:
La Prensa is preoccupied
with the last divorce taking place
with motion picture asses in Hollywood
and while press syndicates cloister themselves
La Prensa and *La Nación* are metaphysical.
Oh what silence from the fat press
when the people are beaten,
but if one of Batista's jackals
is assassinated in Cuba
the presses of our poor America
confess and print their sensational stories,
they lift their hands to their temples,
it is then that they know and publish,

the Sip, Sop, Sep meets
to save the virgins in trouble
and running to their purse in New York
they hurriedly solicit
the constant inducement of money
for the "liberty" they patronize.
And these web-footed men
swarm over Latin America,
they kiss Chamudes[24] in Santiago,
Judas Ravines[25] waits for them in Lima
later enriched and enthused
by that liberty exhaled
from Washington where rock and roll plays,
they dance with Dubois and Gaínza.

XXXVI

Dancing with Blacks

Blacks of the continent, to the New World
you brought what had been missing:
without Blacks drums do not breathe
without Blacks guitars do not play.
Our green America was immobile
until a dance of blood and grace
sprang from a black couple
and it swayed like a palm tree.
And after suffering so much misery
and cutting cane to death
and minding pigs in the woods
and carrying the heaviest rocks
and washing pyramids of clothes
and going upstairs weighted down
and stopping with no one on the road
and having neither plate nor spoon
and earning more beatings than salary
and tolerating the sale of your sister
and grinding flour a whole century
and eating one day a week
and running like a horse all the time
delivering boxes of sandals,
wielding the broom and saw,
digging up roads and mountains,
lying down tired with death,

to live yet again in the morning,
singing like no one else can sing,
singing with body and soul.
My heart, in order to say this,
my life and my words tear apart
and I cannot continue because I prefer
to go with the African palms,
protectresses of terrestrial music
that excites me now from the window:
and I am going to dance on the roads
with my Black brothers in La Habana.

XXXVII

A Professor Disappears

In New York an errant cheese smell
circulates over false gardenias:
from 42nd to Long Island
it covered every wintry thing
and the classroom shivered
between sudden heat and dead cold.
From there the friend emerged surrounded
by air as bitter as his exile,
but Urban North America
had wrapped him up in a new suit
thinking that it could cut him loose from
the ancestral figure of his memory.
Galíndez[26] was the professor's name
and on that night he went to hell.
They hit him on the head
and took him unconscious
through the night, the streets,
the abandoned airport
toward Santo Domingo, where a pale
ruffian with an old face reigns,
a satanic monkey supported
there by the State Department.
And they brought him to the throne,
sad professor with his memories,
it is not known whether he was burned alive
or slowly flayed,

or cut into little pieces,
or roasted in the blood of other dead men,
but before the assembled Court
the professor was taken to his torment:
the pilot was paid right there
(North American of course)
and the tyrant carries on in Santo Domingo.
In New York winter continues.

XXXVIII

The Heroes

In this ship of bloody mire
many were wounded and killed:
the wretched abyss swallowed them
with its tortures and its prisoners.
For this fortress of the cruel
there are bullets and money in Washington
and Trujillo's son is a lover,
for Hollywood, he is a total gentleman.
But the students who shoot
against evil, alone or scattered,
will find no asylum in Embassies
nor will they find ships in port
nor planes to transport them to another place
unless it is to where torments await them.
They will be denied a visa to New York
until the young clandestine hero
is, later, denounced and discovered:
they will leave no eyes in sockets,
one by one they will crush the bones.
Later they will show off at the UN
in this Free World of ours,
while the North American Minister
gives Trujillo new weapons.
This tale is terrible, and if you have suffered
you will forgive me, I do not lament it.
That is how the wicked perpetuate themselves:
this is reality and I do not lie.

XXXIX

North American Friend

Man from the north, North American,
industrial harvester of apples,
simple as a pine in a pine grove,
geographic spruce of Alaska,
Yankee of the villages and factories
with wife, responsibility and children,
fertile engineers who work
in the immutable jungle of numbers
or in the time machine of factories,
workers broad, narrow and bent
over wheels and flames,
dissolute poets who have lost
Whitman's faith in the human race,
I want what I love and hate
to remain clear in my words:
my only rebuke against you
is for the silence that says nothing:
we do not know what North Americans
meditate in their homes,
we understand the sweetness of the family,
but we also love the sudden blaze,
so that when things happen in this world
we want to share your learning
but we find that two or three people
close the North American doors
and only the "Voice of America" is heard
which is like listening to a lean chicken.

But the rest I celebrate here,
your feats of today and tomorrow
and I think that the delayed satellite
that you orbited at dawn
is healthy for the pride of all:
Why always be in first place?
In this contest for life
boasting has forever fallen behind:
thus we can together go to the sun
and drink wine from the same jar.
We are Americans like you
we do not want to exclude you from anything,
but we want to conserve what is ours,
there is lots of space for our souls
we can live without trampling
and with underdeveloped sympathy
until with sincerity we speak
how far we have gone, face to face.
The world is changing and we don't believe
that there must be a victory of bombs and swords.
On this base we will understand each other
without your suffering at all.
We are not going to exploit your petroleum,
we will not intervene with customs,
we will not sell electrical energy
to North American villages:
we are peaceful people who can

be content with the little we earn,
we do not want to submit anyone
to coveting the circumstances of others.
We respect Lincoln's space
and Paul Robeson's clear conscience.
We learned to love with Charlie Chaplin
(although his power was evilly rewarded).
And so many things, the geography
that unites us in the desired land,
everything tells me to say once again
that we are sailing in the same boat:
it could sink with pride:
let us load it with bread and apples,
let us load it with Blacks and Whites,
with understanding and hopes.

XL

Tomorrow Throughout the Caribbean

Unsullied youth of this bloody sea,
young communists of the day:
there will be more of you to clean
this territory of tyrannies,
one day we shall be able to meet,
and in freedom my poetry
will sing once again among you.
Comrades, I await this rejoicing.

XLI

A Song for Sierra Maestra

If silence is asked for when taking leave
of our kin who return to dust,
I am going to ask for a sonorous minute,
for once the whole voice of America,
only one minute of deep song
I ask in the honor of the Sierra Maestra.
Let us forget men for now:
for now let us honor this soil
which hid in its mysterious mountains
the spark that would burn in the prairies.
I celebrate the rough groves,
the tough habitat of the rocks,
the night of indecisive murmurings,
with the flickering of the stars,
the naked silence of forests,
the enigma of people without flags:
until all began to throb,
bursting into flames like a bonfire.
The invincible bearded men came down
to establish peace over the land,
now all is bright but then
all was dark in the Sierra Maestra:
thus I ask for this unanimous minute
to sing this Song of Protest,
I commence with these words
so that they be repeated in America
"Open your eyes offended people
there is a Sierra Maestra everywhere."

MEDITATION OVER
SIERRA MAESTRA

XLII

Written in the Year 2000

I want to speak with the last stars
now, elevated on this human mountain,
I am alone with my companion, night
and a heart spent throughout the years:
I came to this solitude from far,
I have a right to the sovereign dream,
to rest with open eyes
among the eyes of the fatigued,
and while man sleeps with his tribe,
when all eyes are closed,
I let time pass over my face
like obscure air or a tearful heart,
I see what's coming and what's being born,
the pains that were defeated,
the destitute hopes of my people:
the children in school with shoes,
the giving out of bread and justice
as the sun gives out with summer.
I see fulfilled simplicity,
the purity of a man with his plow,
I go and come among the farms
without encountering large plantations.
Light was close but not yet found:
love seemed so distant:
reason was always close:
we were the lost ones
already believing in a sad world
full of emperors and soldiers
when it was suddenly seen that
the cruel and the bad were gone forever

and that everyone was tranquil
at home, on the street, working.
And now it is known it's not good
that the land be in the hands of a few,
that there is no necessity to run
between governors and courts of justice.
How simple peace is and how difficult
assailed by rocks and sticks
every day and night
as if we were no longer Christians.
The night is deep and pure like rock
and it touches my ribs with cold
as if saying sleep quickly,
for your chores are already done.
But I speak to the stars,
speak an obscure and clear language,
converse with the night itself
with simplicity like sister and brother.
The night envelops me with its hands:
I recognize I am that darkness
I left behind in the distant past
when youthful spring
breathed in my provincial dress.
All the love of that time is lost,
the pain of an abducted aroma,
the color of a street with ashes,
the perpetual sky of a few hands!
And later those devouring climates
where my heart was devoured,
the ships that fled without course,

the obscure or lean nations,
the fever I had in Burma
and the love that was crucified.
I am only a man and I carry my pain
like any other mortal weighted down
by loving, loving, loving without being loved
and by not loving once he has been loved.
The ashes of a night emerge
near the sea, in a sacred river,
and a woman's dark cadaver
burning in an abandoned hearth:
the Irrawaddy [27] from the density
moves its sharklike water and light.
The fishermen from Ceylon who with me
raised the whole ocean and its fish
and the nets sprouting miraculous
red velvet fish
while the elephants waited
for me to give an offering with my hands.
Oh how much time accumulated on my
brow like an opaque clock
that bears in its fragile movement
an interminably long thread
that begins with a child who cries
and ends in a wanderer with a sack!
Later war and its pains came
and the dead Spaniards touch my eyes
and search for me in the night,
I look for them, they do not see me,
nevertheless, I see their extinguished light:

Don Antonio [28] dies without hope,
Miguel Hernández [29] dead in his prisons,
poor Federico [30] assassinated
by evil medieval men,
by unloyal multitudes of Paneros [31] :
the assassins of the nightingales.
Oh so much, so much darkness, so much blood
tonight they call me by name:
they now touch me with icy wings,
they show me their enormous martyrdom:
no one has avenged them and they ask it of me.
And only my tenderness knows them.
Oh how much darkness in a night
that does not overflow this celestial cup,
the silence of distances sounds
like an inaccessible seashell
and stars fall into my hands still
filled with music and shadows.
In this space the turbulent weight
of my life neither overcomes nor weeps,
I discharge the pain that visits me
as I release a pigeon:
if there is accounting to be done, it must be done
with what's to come and what's beginning,
with the happiness of all the world
and not with what time crumbles.
And here under the sky of Sierra Maestra
I manage to greet only the dawn
because I was late for my chores,
my life was spent with so many things,

that I leave my work to other hands
and my song will be sung by another mouth.
Because that is how the workday is linked
and the rose will continue blooming.
Man does not falter on his journey:
another takes up mysterious arms:
human rebirth has no end,
the butterfly springs out of winter,
more fragile than a flower,
thus its beauty has no repose
and its colorful wings move
with a radiant congruence.
And one man alone built a door,
taking but a single drop from the sea
until from one life to another
we will raise a happy city
with the arms of those not yet alive.
That is the unity we will achieve:
light organized through shadow,
through the continuity of desire
and the time that passes with the hours
until everyone is content.
Thus History begins once again.
And thus, from the height of these mountains,
far from Chile and its cordilleras
I receive my past in a cup
and I lift it over the entire earth,
and although my country circulates in my blood
without its flow ever stopping
in this hour my night's reasoning

marks in Cuba the common banner
of the obscure hemisphere which awaited
a true victory at last.
I leave it on this summit protected,
high, undulating over the prairies,
representing for the oppressed peoples
the dignity born out of fighting:
Cuba is a clear, upright mast visible
throughout space and darkness,
it is like a tree born in the center
of the Caribbean sea and its ancient sorrows:
its foliage is seen from all parts
and its seeds root themselves in earth,
raising in dark America
the edifice of springtime.

XLIII

Final Judgment

(The Publisher records here that with this title the Poet announces a poem that will close this volume in a definitive edition.)

1964

Pablo Neruda's Funeral

*This narrative was taken from a tape recording of
Neruda's funeral done by Carlos Ortiz Tejada; it was written
by Ricardo Garibay, and translated by Mauricio Schoijet. It is
reprinted by permission of* University Review. *Copyright 1973,
Entelechy Press Corp.*

The funeral procession begins at the poet's house,
where the corpse was lying in state attended by his widow and
sisters. The wake is held in the middle of a muddy, flooded
room that was once his library. Books and documents are
floating in the mud along with furniture. The day before, a
stream was diverted into the house by the military who
smashed everything in sight with their rifle butts and left the
house flooded.

The coffin has been removed and is being carried by
some friends of the poet. Only a few people are present
accompanying his widow and sisters and the Mexican
Ambassador, Martinez Corbala.

Someone inquires and is told, "Pablo Neruda."
"What?" "Yes, sir, Pablo Neruda." And quietly the word
spreads, and the name opens doors and windows, it begins to
appear at half-closed shops, it descends from telephone poles
with the workers who worked on them, it stops buses and it
empties them, brings out people running from distant streets,
people who arrive already crying, still hoping it is not true.
The name keeps emerging, like a miracle of anger, in
hundreds and hundreds of people—men, women, children
almost all poor, almost all people of the shantytowns of
Santiago—each of them becoming Pablo Neruda.

We hear a grayish noise of ordinary shoes, we smell the infinite dust, we feel on our eyes the strained breathing of thousands of throats that are ready to explode.

Then we hear a sound: shy, half choked, prayed in secret—"Comrade Pablo Neruda"—and we hear an answer of someone who is saying, "Don't tell that I said it," here now and forever.

A voice shouts, "Comrade Pablo Neruda!" and there, already in anger, "Here!"—already throwing a hat, stepping firmly and facing the military who are approaching and surrounding the crowd.

And here begins something that we imagined ancient and monumental, something from the realm of great literature, something incredible, necessarily fantastic, because it belonged to pure thought and would never appear in the flesh at a street corner. Some kind of giant litany for who knows how many dead. Who knows how many more murdered people this litany is for? A remote voice, shrill voice, howls in a bestial, heartbreaking way, "Comrade Pablo Neruda!" And a choir watched by millions of assassins, by millions of informers, sings "Here, with us, now and forever!"

There, farther, here, on the right, on the left, at the end of the marching column, a column of three thousand, the Chilean cries rise up, twists of an inexhaustible womb of sadness, twinges of light: "Comrade Pablo Neruda!" "Comrade Pablo Neruda!" "Comrade Pablo Neruda!" "Comrade Salvador Allende!" "Here!" "Here!" "Here, with us, now and forever!" "Chilean people, they are stepping on you, they are assassinating you, they are torturing you!"

"Chilean people, don't give up, the revolution is awaiting us, we'll fight until we finish with the henchmen!"

Swirls of crying, swearings, threats, wailings, of darkness at noon, of voices choking with anger. Hellish vocabulary, crazy, heavenly words. Three thousand overwhelmingly defeated people are howling.

And suddenly, howling powerfully, a woman begins to sing Neruda's verses. Her voice grows suddenly alone, "I have been reborn many times, from the depths/of defeated stars. . ." and all shout, all, they shout from their memories ". . . reconstructing the threats/of eternities that I populated with my hands. . . ."

NOTES

1. Luis Muñoz Marín: Governor of Puerto Rico (1949-1964).
2. Augusto César Sandino organized resistance against presence of U.S. marines in Nicaragua. Killed February, 1933.
3. Rubén Darío: (1867-1916) poet born in Nicaragua.
4. General Rafael Leonídas Trujillo: dictator of the Dominican Republic (1930-1961).
5. José Martí: (1853-1895). Cuban orator who led Cuba's revolution from Spain in 1895.
6. Batista ruled Cuba 1952-1958.
7. Ubico: dictator of Guatemala 1931-1944.
8. Anastasio Somoza: leader of militia which took charge after the departure of U.S. marines from Nicaragua. Became President 1936. Assassinated 1956.
9. Araucanian: Indians of southern Chile contemporaneous with the Inca. Remained unconquered until late nineteenth century.
10. Pedro de Valdivia: a sixteenth century Spanish conquistador who was executed by the Araucanians.
11. Jacobo Arbenz Guzmán: established communist government in Guatemala in 1950. Overthrown through CIA intervention in 1954.
12. Martinez ruled El Salvador 1931-1944.
13. Orinoco: Venezuelan river. Simón Bolívar used the river basin as his base for the resistance against Spain.
14. Mariano Picón Salas: (1901-1965) prolific Venezuelan prose writer, critic, and historian, who spent many years of exile in Chile.

15. Juan Vicente Gómez: Venezuelan dictator (1908–1935), during whose administration oil was discovered off the Venezuelan coast.
16. Joaquín Gabaldón Marquez: Venezuelan writer who lived through and wrote about the "Generation of '28," a revolutionary group harshly suppressed by Gómez.
17. Medina Angarita ruled Venezuela 1941–1945.
18. Rómulo Gallegos: novelist elected President of Venezuela in 1947.
19. Pérez Jiménez ruled Venezuela 1951–1958.
20. Rómulo Betancourt: President of Venezuela 1959–1963.
21. La Coubre: a French ship carrying armaments which exploded in the Havana harbor March 3, 1960.
22. Juan Perón: ruled Argentina from 1946–1955.
23. Gaínza Paz: publisher of *La Prensa,* Buenos Aires.
24. Marcos Chamudes: Chilean news commentator.
25. Eudocio Ravines: Peruvian writer of anti-Fidel Castro pamphlets. Jules Dubois: anti-Castro news reporter.
26. Jesus de Galíndez: a Basque writer who planned to publish a book criticizing Trujillo.
27. Irrawaddy: a river in Burma.
28. Antonio Machado: (1875–1939) Spanish poet who died in exile in France.
29. Miguel Hernández: (1910–1942) Spanish poet who died in one of Franco's prisons.
30. Federico García Lorca: (1899–1936) Spanish poet and playwright executed at the outset of the Spanish Civil War.
31. Leopoldo Panero: Establishment Spanish poet.

Notes Prepared by Richard August